DEBE... to Colchester
School ... died scientific
and ... ses Dorling
Kinde... birth of her
childr... ren's books.

is th... coln ... Sieveking
and *B*... ey, Australia.

Please return/renew this item by the last date shown
Thank you for using your library

FIFE COUNCIL LIBRARIES

For my own special family

Costumes designed by Katrina Meletopolou
Design and art direction by Debbie MacKinnon
Thank you to all the lovely children who acted out the story:
Alena, Amelia, Anja, Avalon, Chloe, Elliot, Fabian, James,
Lyndon, Marlon, Nayibe, Patrick, Scott, Timothy, Thomas, Verity

Away in a Manger copyright © Frances Lincoln Limited 2000
Text copyright © Debbie MacKinnon 2000
Photographs copyright © Debbie MacKinnon 2000
Music arrangements © Barrie Carson Turner 1993

First published in Great Britain in 2000 by
Frances Lincoln Limited, 4 Torriano Mews,
Torriano Avenue, London NW5 2RZ
www.franceslincoln.com

First paperback edition 2002

British Library Cataloguing in Publication Data available on request

ISBN 0-7112-1666-5

Printed in Hong Kong

1 3 5 7 9 8 6 4 2

Away
in a
Manger

**The Christmas Story
retold by Debbie MacKinnon**

Photographs by Andre Martin

FRANCES LINCOLN

A lena, Marlon and Patrick are very excited. So are Tom and Amelia, Fabian, Elliot, Nayibe and Anja. Nobody can keep still, everyone is jumping around and chattering.

"Where's my halo?"

"I've lost the frankincense but here are the crooks..."

"Keep still Nayibe, while I fix your wings!"

"Hold on to that lamb, Tom!"

"Where shall we put the manger?"

The children are getting dressed up to tell you the wonderful story of Christmas.

"Now, are you all ready?
The story is about to begin..."

Long, long ago, a young woman called Mary lived in the village of Nazareth. She was about to marry Joseph, a kind man who worked as a carpenter.

One day, as Mary was busy around the house, a shining angel appeared before her. The angel had come with a very special message. "Do not be afraid, Mary," said the angel. "God is sending you a son and His name shall be Jesus."

Mary was very happy and excited that God had chosen her to be the mother of His son.

S oon Mary and Joseph were married, but before the baby was born, they had to leave their house in Nazareth and travel far away to Bethlehem, where Joseph had been born. The Roman emperor had ordered that everyone must return to the town of their birth to be counted and pay their taxes.

It was a long and tiring journey. When they finally arrived, Bethlehem was packed with crowds of people. There was no room for Mary and Joseph to stay at the inn.

Mary knew it was nearly time for her baby to be born and she felt very weary.

"Look, you can shelter in the stable with the animals," said the innkeeper. "At least you will be warm and dry in there."

Mary was glad to rest at last.

That night Mary's baby son was born in the stable.

"Welcome, Jesus," whispered His mother as she wrapped Him up and gently laid the baby in a manger to sleep.

Nearby, some shepherds were watching their sheep in the fields. Suddenly a dazzling angel appeared out of the darkness and all the shepherds were terrified. "Fear not," said the angel, "I bring you good tidings of great joy.

"Today a baby has been born in Bethlehem and He will be your saviour, Christ the Lord. You will find the baby wrapped up and lying in a manger." At once, the sky was full of light and angels singing, "Glory to God in the highest, and on earth peace, goodwill toward men."

In an instant, the angels were gone, the sky was dark again, and the shepherds were alone. "We must go and find the baby," they said to each other in wonder.

So they hurried into Bethlehem, leaving their sheep alone on the hillside, taking only a newborn lamb with them as a gift. They found Jesus in the stable with Mary and Joseph just as the angel had told them.

The shepherds knelt down to look at the sleeping child, saying, "Praise the Lord!"

Then they quietly slipped away to tell the wonderful news to everyone they met.

Far, far away, three Wise Men were studying the night sky, when they noticed a bright new glittering star in the east. Balthazar, Caspar and Melchior knew that this was a sign that a great king had been born, and so they set out to follow the star. They travelled onwards for many long days and nights, until finally the star led them to Bethlehem, where Jesus lay.

"We have come to see the new king," the Wise Men said, rejoicing that they had found the baby at last. Then they knelt down to worship Him, and brought out gifts fit for a king – gold, frankincense and myrrh.

Everyone was full of joy at the birth of Jesus.

Away in a Manger

lit - tle Lord Je - sus a - - sleep on the hay.

The cattle are lowing, the baby awakes,
But little Lord Jesus, no crying he makes.
I love thee Lord Jesus. Look down from the sky,
And stay by my side until morning is nigh.

How to stage the Nativity

The photographs in this book provide lots of ideas for putting on your own nativity play. The costumes are simply made, using one basic pattern for the robes. Find a simple pattern for a loose 'A' line dress or nightdress. You can adjust the length and sleeves to suit the children involved in the play. Neaten edges with bias binding, and fasten them at the back.
Be adaptable and find materials from markets or charity shops; consider recycling unwanted items such as old curtains or tablecloths! Raid the Christmas decoration box and find treasures in your sewing basket: old buttons, braid, sequins or sparkly costume jewellery can all be used to great effect in the costumes. A craft glue gun would be very useful for attaching decorations.

What you need:

★ MARY
- Long dress with sleeves, (from basic pattern).
- Square shawl (this can be used later to wrap the infant Jesus).
- Dark blue cloak to contrast with dress.
- Basket of twigs and small brush.

★ JOSEPH
- Long robe (from basic pattern).
- Loose draw-string trousers, or old pair of track-suit bottoms in dark colour.
- Square of light fabric (we used dyed cheese-cloth) or even a tea towel, for headdress.
- Strip of cord or plaited fabric for head band.
- Staff for his journey – bamboo with a raffia trim.
- Old canvas or raffia travel bag.

★ INNKEEPER
- Robe (from basic pattern).
- Apron in contrast fabric (with pocket).
- Large old key on cord to go around neck.
- Lantern.

★ SHEPHERDS
- Robes in a variety of plain colours in coarse textured fabric (from basic pattern).
- Contrast colour neckerchiefs – bought or made.
- Large squares of cheese-cloth for headdresses.
- Strips of cord or plaited fabric for headbands.
- Cords with tassels to tie around waists of robes.
- Toy lamb (or real one if available!).

Shepherds' crooks: cut a thick stick of bamboo to a suitable length for each child. Bend a long piece of thick flexible craft wire in half. Wind the open ends around the bamboo to secure. Bend the other end into a hooked crook shape. Wind raffia around the crook to disguise the join between bamboo and wire and secure.

★ WISE MEN
- Robes in rich fabric (from basic pattern).
- Loose baggy trousers in suitable colours to match/contrast with robes.
- Cut down ladies' leggings or adapt track-suit bottoms in dark colours.
- Selection of richly patterned scarves, saris, embroidered dressing gowns, colourful fringing, scraps of velvet and silky fabrics. Use these to wrap around kings as drapes or stoles.

Headdresses for Wise Men: take three old baseball caps and remove peaks. Wrap pieces of fabric around the caps and secure to create turbans. Wrap more fabric around strips of foam or wadding to create broad padded brims. Secure to headdresses. Add 'jewels', ribbons, feathers and decorations.

Gifts for Wise Men: 1. Spray a bottle with paint and add jewels. 2. Paint an old box in gold and add jewels for decoration. Fill with gold tinsel and ropes of gold coloured beads. 3. Find a suitable pot with a lid and decorate. Alternatively, wrap three different shaped gifts in shiny paper.

★ ANGEL GABRIEL

· Long robe with wide sleeves in light-coloured silky fabric (from basic pattern).
· Wide strip of contrast colour fabric – drape across robe and attach at shoulder and waist with a few stitches.
· Decorative braid for neck and sleeves.
· Tinsel or stars wound onto hairband for halo.
· Large wings *(see separate instructions below)*.

★ HOST OF ANGELS

· Sleeveless dresses in a variety of pale silky fabrics (from basic pattern).
· Tinsel or stars wound onto hairbands for haloes.
· Wings, sprayed silver or gold *(see intructions below)*.
· Musical instruments for the angels to 'play'.
· Harp made from cut-out foam board, sprayed gold, with thin silver cord 'strings' and Christmas cherub decorations *(see photo above)*.

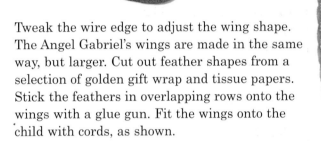

Angels' wings: make a pattern using the photo below as a guide. Cut out the shape from one piece of very thin, flexible foam rubber. Attach thick pliable craft wire to top edge of wings and secure with strong thread. Spray wings on both sides with gold or silver paint – allow to dry. Glue stars or sequins to top of wings. Attach decorative cord, with glue gun or stitches, to top edges of wings, covering the wire. Sew a further metre of cord down the centre panel of the wings making a loop at the bottom edge, this is to attach the wings to the child. Take each cord across the child's shoulders to the opposite loop, back through the loop, and then bring to the front of the costume and tie together above the waist. The wings should sit quite high up on the child's shoulders.

Tweak the wire edge to adjust the wing shape. The Angel Gabriel's wings are made in the same way, but larger. Cut out feather shapes from a selection of golden gift wrap and tissue papers. Stick the feathers in overlapping rows onto the wings with a glue gun. Fit the wings onto the child with cords, as shown.

BACKDROP AND PROPS

Attach different sized silver stars to a dark blue curtain or painted backdrop. Add one larger golden star. Recycle old Christmas decorations, buy stars from a party shop, or cut out your own from silver foil. Arrange several bales of straw or hay on the stage for the children to sit or stand on. Make a manger from a base of bamboo sticks tied together with raffia, or recycle an old cane laundry basket. Fill the manger with hay. Use a life-sized baby doll for the infant Jesus. Wrap the baby in Mary's shawl.

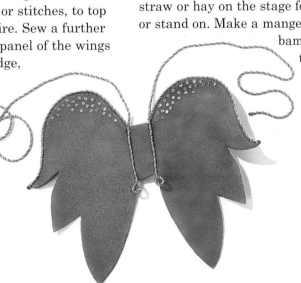

MORE TITLES IN PAPERBACK
FROM FRANCES LINCOLN

BABIES' FAVOURITES
Debbie MacKinnon
Illustrated by Lisa Kopper

Toddlers will love lifting up the flaps and talking about their favourite
things in this gentle rhyming book with lively illustrations.

ISBN 0-7112-2070-0

AN ANGEL JUST LIKE ME
Mary Hoffman
Illustrated by Cornelius Van Wright & Ying-Hwa Hu

When Tyler picks up the broken Christmas-tree angel, he can't help asking,
"Why are they always pink? Aren't there any black angels?"
When he goes shopping for a black angel, he can't find
a single one – until he tells his friend Carl the problem.

ISBN 0-7112-1309-7

THE SNOW WHALE
Caroline Pitcher
Illustrated by Jackie Morris

One November morning, when the hills are hump-backed with snow,
Laurie and Leo decide to build a snow whale. As they shovel,
pat and polish to bring the snow whale out of the hill,
the whale gradually takes on a life of its own.

ISBN 0-7112-1093-4

Frances Lincoln titles are available from all good bookshops.
You can also buy books and find out more about your favourite titles,
authors and illustrators at our website: www.franceslincoln.com.